OLIVER CROMWELL

LEON ASHWORTH

CHERRYTREE BOOKS

A Cherrytree Book

Designed and produced by
A S Publishing

First published 1997
by Cherrytree Press Ltd
a subsidiary of
The Chivers Company Ltd
Windsor Bridge Road
Bath BA2 3AX

British Library Cataloguing in Publication Data

Ashworth, Leon
    Oliver Cromwell. – (British history makers)
    1. Cromwell, Oliver – Juvenile literature
    2.Heads of State – Great Britain – Biography – Juvenile
        literature
    3. Great Britain – History – Puritan Revolution, 1642-1660 –
        Juvenile literature
    I. Title
    941'.064'092

ISBN 0 7451 5287 2 (Hardcover)
ISBN 0 7540 9010 8 (Softcover)

Printed and bound in Italy by New Interlitho, Milan

Acknowledgments
Design: Richard Rowan
Editorial: John Grisewood
Artwork: Malcolm Porter
Photographs: *Barnaby's Picture Library* 11 bottom, 17 top left, 25 bottom left &
right, 28 bottom *The Bridgeman Art Library* 5, 7 left & right (Walker Art
Gallery, Liverpool), 8/9 bottom, 10 top & bottom, 12 bottom left (Collection
of the Earl of Pembroke, Wilton House), 14 top & bottom, 15 bottom, 16
bottom, 17 bottom, 19 bottom, 20 bottom left (The Fine Art Society,
London), 21 bottom (York City Art Gallery), 22/23 top, 24 top, 26/27
bottom *The Cromwell Museum* 8 bottom left & right, 24 bottom left *Lambeth
Palace Library* 21 top *The Mansell Collection* 11 top, 12 centre right, 13 centre
left & top right, 23 top right *Mary Evans Picture Library* Cover portrait (1 &
24 bottom right), 4 bottom, 6 top, 8 top, 9 top, 12/13 bottom, 15 centre, 16
centre, 17 top right, 18 bottom left & right, 19 top, 20 bottom right, 24/25
top, 25 top right, 26 top left, 27 top right *Milton's Cottage Museum* 28 top
right *National Portrait Gallery* 27 top left, 29 centre left *Palace of
Westminster* 29 bottom centre *Robert Harding Picture Library* 29 centre
right *Victoria & Albert Museum* 23 bottom *Zefa Pictures* 29 top right

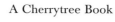

CONTENTS

■ OLIVER CROMWELL ■

OLIVER CROMWELL ruled Britain as lord protector from 1653 to 1658. For these few years, the country had no king or queen but was governed as a republic that was known as the Commonwealth.

Cromwell came to power because he was a general on the side of parliament in the Civil War against King Charles I. He helped to defeat the king and was one of the parliamentary leaders who signed the order for the king's execution.

WARTS AND ALL

Some people thought Cromwell a good man; others feared him as a cruel tyrant. When an artist was painting his portrait, Cromwell told him to paint his 'warts and everything'.

Cromwell was a Puritan. Puritans were a group of Christians who believed in a plain, simple form of worship. They disagreed with the ceremonies and some of the beliefs of both the Roman Catholic Church and the Church of England.

A SOLDIER AND STATESMAN

Cromwell had a strong personality, an iron will and a hot temper. He was respected abroad as a strong, patriotic ruler. He tried to govern his country well after many years of civil war, but his harsh methods caused anger, especially in Ireland. When Cromwell died, few people were sad and most welcomed the return of the monarchy soon after Cromwell's death.

CROMWELL'S LIFE

1599 Cromwell born.
1617 Leaves Cambridge University; father dies.
1620 Marries Elizabeth Bourchier.
1628 Becomes MP for Huntingdon. Becomes Puritan.
1639 Eldest son, Robert, dies.
1640 Becomes MP for Cambridge.
1642 Civil War begins. Fights at battle of Edgehill.
1644 Leads cavalry at Marston Moor.
1645 Wins battle of Naseby.
1649 King Charles I executed.
1650 Becomes commander in chief of the army.
1653 Becomes lord protector.
1657 Refuses title of king.
1658 Dies.

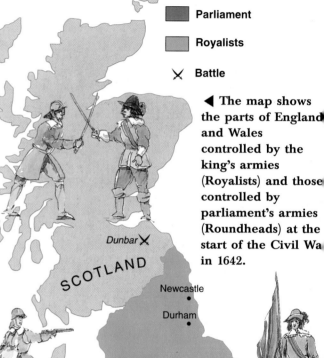

CIVIL WAR 1642

Parliament

Royalists

✕ Battle

◄ The map shows the parts of England and Wales controlled by the king's armies (Royalists) and those controlled by parliament's armies (Roundheads) at the start of the Civil War in 1642.

SCOTLAND

Dunbar ✕

Newcastle

Durham

York
✕ Marston Moor
✕
Preston

Chester
Nottingham
Lincoln

Leicester

✕ Naseby

WALES

Worcester ✕ ✕ Edgehill

ENGLAND

Oxford
ROYALIST HQ

Pembroke

Donnington
✕
Bristol
Newbury
London
PARLIAMENT'S HQ

Exeter

Plymouth

Corfe ✕

▼ Oliver Cromwell's signature.

QUOTES

Cromwell said that he would far rather have *'a plain russet-coated captain that knows what he fights for and loves what he knows than that which you call a "gentleman" and is nothing else'*.

A fellow MP said that Cromwell wore a suit of *'plain cloth which seemed to have been made by an ill country tailor'*.

When someone asked Cromwell's cousin, John Hampden, who *'that sloven'* was, he replied that Cromwell *'hath no ornament in his speech; but . . . should it ever come to a breach with the king (which God forbid!) . . . that sloven will be the greatest man in England'*.

■ CROMWELL'S ENGLAND ■

OLIVER CROMWELL was born in the quiet country town of Huntingdon on 25 April 1599. Queen Elizabeth I had been England's ruler for more than 40 years. The country was growing stronger and richer. In London, theatre-goers cheered two new plays – *As You Like It* and *Henry V* – by William Shakespeare.

WARS OF RELIGION

England had been at war with Spain on and off since the 1560s. Spain was the leader of Catholic Europe. England was Protestant. The two countries were also rivals for trade and colonies overseas. The defeat of the Spanish Armada in 1588 saved England from invasion, but left many Protestants and Catholics in England fearful

▲ Making hay while the sun shines: England was becoming rich and powerful, but for farming people like the Cromwells, daily life changed little.

▼At the beginning of the 17th century, Europe was divided by religious differences.

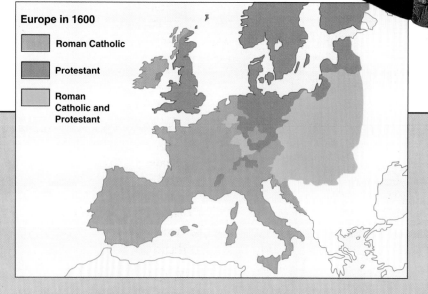

Europe in 1600

- Roman Catholic
- Protestant
- Roman Catholic and Protestant

RELIGIOUS DISPUTES

CROMWELL grew up in a time of religious disputes. Christians in Europe had been quarrelling ever since the early 1500s. In 1517, a German monk called Martin Luther had protested against the way the church was run. This split the church and began the Protestant movement known as the Reformation. In 1534, Henry VIII declared himself head of the Church of England. In France, a civil war between Catholics and Protestants ended the year before Cromwell was born.

▶ In 1605 Guy Fawkes and his fellow Catholic plotters tried to blow up the king and parliament.

Bates, Robert Winter, Christopher Wright, John Wright, Thomas Percy, Guido Fawkes, Robert Catesby, Thomas Winter

◄ James VI of Scotland became James I of England when Elizabeth I died. Charles I also ruled both countries.

▲ Oliver Cromwell was born at the end of Elizabeth I's 'glorious' reign, during which England and the arts had flourished.

of one another. Religious quarrels between Protestants and Catholics were at the root of wars in Europe and conflicts in England.

THE CROMWELLS

Oliver Cromwell's family were Protestants. His parents were called Robert and Elizabeth. Robert owned farmland and was a member of parliament. Both parents came from families that gained land and wealth after King Henry VIII – Queen Elizabeth's father – had closed down Catholic monasteries.

The Cromwells' Huntingdon home had once belonged to a community of nuns. Oliver's grandfather had entertained Queen Elizabeth herself there. The neighbours were mostly farmers and market day was about the only excitement.

■ THE YOUNG CROMWELL ■

OLIVER WENT TO the local grammar school in Huntingdon, where his schoolmaster was a stern Puritan. The boy seems to have enjoyed games more than study – 'tennis, wrestling, running, swimming, handling weapons and riding'.

In 1616 Oliver went to Cambridge University. Here he was noted as a keen player of 'football, cudgels or any other boisterous game or sport'. His student days were cut short by the death of his father in 1617. Oliver had to return home to look after the estate he had inherited. Fortunately, his father had left his mother comfortably off and Oliver was later able to go to Lincoln's Inn in London, to study law.

▲ Dr Thomas Beard, master of Huntingdon Grammar School, was a Puritan and taught Cromwell the same ideals.

LOVE AND MARRIAGE

In London, Oliver fell in love with Elizabeth Bourchier. Her father, Sir James Bourchier, was a wealthy merchant. But he was happy for his eldest daughter to marry a young lawyer from the country.

Elizabeth and Oliver married on 22 August 1620. They remained devoted to each other all their lives. The couple made their home in Huntingdon, where six of their eight children were born. Cromwell lived the life of a country gentleman. He managed the family lands, and in his spare time enjoyed hawking and hunting. He also enjoyed playing dice in the local tavern.

▼ Cromwell's mother, Elizabeth Steward, came from a rich landowning family.

▼ Cromwell's wife, Elizabeth Bourchier, was the daughter of a wealthy London merchant.

THE PURITANS

THE PURITANS were Protestants who believed that God spoke personally to them, so they did not need priests to interpret God's message. They wanted to 'purify' the church, ridding it of rich robes and elaborate rituals. God-fearing and hardworking, the Puritans lived by strict standards of behaviour. They disliked ornaments at home or in church. They disapproved of games on Sunday and going to plays. Some Puritans left England because they were not allowed to practise their religion freely. Many supported parliament during the Civil War.

▼ These Puritans trudging to church through the snow are American settlers.

▶ Oliver Cromwell felt most at home in the country among his farmer friends. Although a firm Puritan, he enjoyed country sports such as hawking and shooting.

THE GOOD LIFE

Cromwell was at home in the country. He did not like what he had seen of London, with its inns and theatres, and fine lords and ladies. He felt comfortable among his farmer-friends, some of whom were Puritans and believed the world was full of 'vanity and badness'.

■ CROMWELL AND THE KING ■

I N 1628 Cromwell was elected a member of parliament. About this time, he had a powerful religious experience. To him, it was like coming 'from darkness into light'.

In 1629, a year after Cromwell entered parliament, the king dissolved it by telling all the members to go home. Charles I had been king for four years and believed that the power of a king was God-given and absolute. If parliament would not do as he wished, by raising taxes, for example, then the king had the right to dismiss it.

Cromwell went home to look after his lands. However, he was now on the side of those people who wanted to shrink the powers of the king.

EVENTS

1629 *Charles I dismisses parliament and rules alone.*
1633 *William Laud becomes archbishop of Canterbury.*
1637 *John Hampden refuses to pay the 'ship money' tax.*
1640 *In the new 'Short Parliament', Cromwell sits as MP for Cambridge. Charles goes to war with the Scots. When parliament refuses to grant him more money, he dismisses it. Charles is forced to call a new parliament, known as the Long Parliament (because it was not dismissed until 1660). The king has to agree to new limits on his powers.*

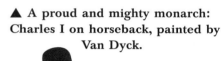

▲ A proud and mighty monarch: Charles I on horseback, painted by Van Dyck.

▼ Charles I tries to arrest five members of the House of Commons in January 1642.

KING AND PARLIAMENT

CHARLES I (seen right opening parliament in 1642) fought wars against France, Spain and Scotland. Scotland still had a separate parliament, and the Scots disagreed with the king over religious questions. Wars cost money, which the king had to find from taxes. Ship money was an old tax paid by coastal towns for defences such as forts and ships. While he ruled without parliament (from 1629 to 1640), Charles ordered inland towns to pay the tax as well. This angered people who believed the king must have parliament's agreement for new taxes.

▼ John Pym and John Hampden were two of the five members of the House of Commons that Charles tried to arrest. The others were Denzil Holles, William Strode and Sir Arthur Haselrig.

John Pym

John Hampden

RETURNING TO POLITICS

In 1639 Cromwell's eldest son Robert died. Deeply saddened, he turned to politics again. In 1640 he went back to the new parliament as MP for Cambridge.

By now, he was respected across eastern England. He also had important friends and relatives. His cousin John Hampden refused to pay ship money (see panel above). This angered the king and Hampden had to go to court, where he lost his case. But Cromwell and other country landowners backed him.

TRIAL OF STRENGTH

Parliament and king were set to collide. John Pym from Somerset was leader of what became known as the Long Parliament that met in 1640. Pym urged members like Cromwell to help reduce the king's power, once and for all.

The king asked for money to pay for a war with Scotland. In return, parliament demanded no more 'king's rule' and called for the arrest of two of the king's closest advisers, Archbishop Laud and the Earl of Strafford.

Charles then tried to arrest Pym, Hampden and three other members of parliament. He went to the House of Commons, but the Commons refused to hand them over. This was open defiance. Fearing he had lost control of London, Charles moved north to Nottingham. On 22 August 1642, he called on all loyal subjects to join him against his enemies. Civil war had begun.

■ PEOPLE AT WAR ■

ALTHOUGH CROMWELL had no training as a soldier, he knew about horses. When the fighting began, he gathered volunteers to form a troop of cavalry (horse soldiers). He also began rounding up good horses for the parliamentary army from farms in eastern England.

THE COUNTRY DIVIDED
At the start of the war,

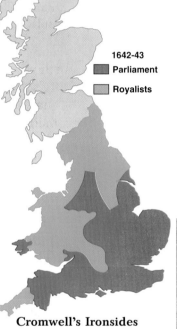

1642-43
Parliament
Royalists

▼ Prince Rupert, nephew of Charles I, was dashing and brave. He commanded the king's cavalry and won many victories. In the end he was defeated by

Cromwell's Ironsides at Marston Moor in 1644.

ROUNDHEADS AND CAVALIERS

EACH side had an insulting nickname for the other. Parliament's men were called Roundheads, because some ordinary soldiers had short haircuts (unlike the ringlets of the upper classes). The king's followers were known as Royalists or Cavaliers. This name came from the Spanish

caballeros (horsemen), and was meant to suggest that they were in the pay of the Catholic king of Spain.

▼ Cavalier soldiers (below left) and Roundheads (below). Since neither side had a uniform, both looked much the same, with similar dress and weapons. In battle they wore signs to recognize each other, such as orange scarves or beanstalks.

▲ A cartoon of 1642 shows the Cavalier dog, Puddle, and the Roundhead dog, Pepper, growling insults at one another.

people in the north and west of England were mainly on the king's side. Charles made Oxford his headquarters. The south (including London) and east sided with parliament. Parliament controlled the ports and the navy, and could stop any soldiers coming from abroad to help Charles.

INTO BATTLE

Cromwell led his soldiers into battle for the first time on 23 October 1642 at Edgehill in Warwickshire. The result was a draw. Both sides returned to their camps as rain and mud brought an end to fighting for the winter. In the countryside, most people cared more about tending their crops and livestock than marching off to fight.

WAR OF WORDS

News of the war spread slowly. Each side put its case in books, news-sheets and pamphlets. Alongside the arguments they published cartoons that savagely mocked the other side.

Being king gave Charles an advantage. To fight against the monarch seemed a treasonous and dangerous thing to do – unless, like Cromwell, you had strong convictions.

◄Prince Rupert in action at Edgehill. Despite his valour, the battle was drawn.

■ CROMWELL THE SOLDIER ■

THE ROYALISTS THOUGHT they had the better army. The daring Prince Rupert of the Rhine led the king's cavalry. Rupert was Charles's nephew. Now 23, he had been a soldier since he was 14 and had fought in battles in Europe. He knew that soldiers on horses could travel swiftly across England, where there were few large forests, rivers or mountains.

Although they carried pistols, cavalrymen used swords for most fighting. Armies had cannon pulled by horses, but the big guns were clumsy and fired slowly. Cannon were most useful for knocking down the walls of towns or castles.

STANDING FAST

Before battle, infantry or foot-soldiers lined up in rows, with the cavalry grouped to the sides. Many foot-soldiers were pikemen, whose spear-like weapons were more than three times a man's height. Rows of bristling pikes could keep enemy horsemen at a distance and force a way through enemy lines.

▲ Queen Henrietta Maria, Charles I's wife, flees from pursuing Roundheads. A French princess and a Catholic, she helped her husband by raising money for him abroad and gathering troops.

1644
■ Parliament
■ Royalists

▼ 'And when did you last see your father?' In this famous Victorian painting, Roundheads who have taken over a Royalist house question the owner's son.

Musketeers fired their guns (which were like one-shot rifles) at close range. They stood fast in the face of beating drums and the thunder of horses' hooves as the enemy rode at them out of the dust and cannon smoke.

A NEW ARMY

Cromwell talked parliament into forming a new army strong enough to march from the eastern counties to attack the Royalists in the north and west. He demanded that its officers should be good commanders. The new army was formed in the spring of 1644. It was led by the Earl of Manchester, with Cromwell as second-in-command.

VICTORY IN THE NORTH

The Scots had chosen to fight on the side of parliament and their troops joined the Roundheads to attack the city of York. Prince Rupert dashed north to help the Royalists, and the two armies met on Marston Moor, near York, in July 1644. Cromwell's cavalry, nicknamed 'Ironsides' by Rupert, won the day. The north of England was under parliament's control.

Cromwell had proved himself a brave leader, but he thought that the Earl of Manchester was not a bold enough general. He backed Sir Thomas Fairfax as the army's new commander.

SOLDIERS IN UNIFORM

IN THE early part of the Civil War, soldiers on both sides wore the same kind of clothes. Then parliament's New Model Army soldiers began wearing red uniforms. Uniforms helped soldiers to tell who was who in the muddle of battle. Royalists wore more showy clothes, especially the cavalry, and some men wore their hair long. Some soldiers wore armour: a pikeman wore a metal breastplate and helmet. A musketeer (right) wore no armour.

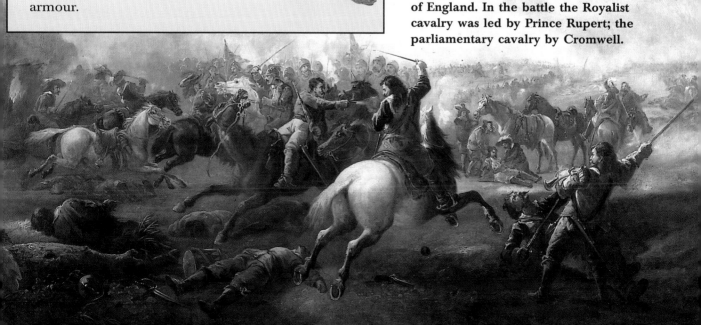

▼ Parliament's victory at Marston Moor in 1644 led to the fall of York and the collapse of the Royalist cause in the north of England. In the battle the Royalist cavalry was led by Prince Rupert; the parliamentary cavalry by Cromwell.

■ PARLIAMENT WINS ■

AFTER HIS PART in the victory at Marston Moor, Cromwell got his way. Another new army – the New Model Army – was organized, led by General Fairfax.

Discipline was strict but the men had regular pay. Before this, unpaid soldiers had stolen food and money from the villages they passed through, and looted the wagons and bodies of the defeated enemy in the hope of finding money or jewels.

THE BATTLE OF NASEBY

In June 1645, Cavaliers and Roundheads faced each other near the Northamptonshire village of Naseby. The day began well for the king, as the greatly outnumbered Royalists drove off some of the Roundhead cavalry. However, Cromwell kept his Ironsides together and while the Cavalier horsemen chased the enemy across country, he and Fairfax attacked the king's foot-soldiers until they broke ranks and fled. Among the captured stores, the Roundheads found bread and cheese for supper. It was the first meal that day for most of them.

Parliament's army moved on to

EVENTS

1645 Venice (at this time an independent state) fights a war with Turkey. The magic lantern is invented. Battle of Naseby is won by parliament. Archbishop Laud is executed.

1646 Oxford is taken by parliament. The king is imprisoned. He refuses to agree to parliament's demands for reform.

1645

■ Parliament

□ Royalists

▶ Charles dictates a message to his secretary. The king sometimes wrote in code, but even so his captured letters were used as evidence against him at his trial.

SIEGE!

EACH SIDE in the Civil War laid siege to the other side's strongholds. To attack a fortress like Corfe Castle in Dorset (below), the army camped around it. Starved of supplies and fresh troops, the people inside sometimes gave up without a fight. If not, the besiegers fired cannon at the stone walls, to make a hole. Barrels of gunpowder were then placed against the weakened walls, to blow them up. Once a wall was breached, soldiers rushed through to fight hand-to-hand with pistols and swords. Corfe Castle was reduced to ruins by the parliamentarians after a six-week siege in 1646 failed to break the will of its defender, Lady Bankes.

▼ The two armies face each other before the battle of Naseby on 14 June 1645. This was the first big test for parliament's New Model Army.

▶ General Thomas Fairfax, commander of the New Model Army, with his military council.

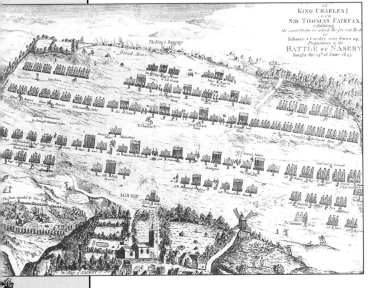

KING CHARLES I
AND
SIR THOMAS FAIRFAX
exhibiting
the exact Order in which the several Bodies
or
Infantry & Cavalry were drawn up.
Preparatory to the
BATTLE of NASEBY
fought the 14th of June 1645.

▼ Cromwell leads his troops and prisoners after his victory at the battle of Naseby. In the battle, the Royalists were ill-equipped and outnumbered by 9000 to 14,000 men. Soon 'there was not a man or horse of the king's army to be seen except the prisoners'.

attack the Royalist strongholds of Newark and Oxford. In 1646, King Charles fled and gave himself up to the Scots, who handed him over to parliament.

CHARLES TAKEN CAPTIVE

The king was a prisoner, but still the monarch. Cromwell hoped that he and other army leaders could agree a peaceful settlement with Charles. Cromwell was tired of fighting and worried that things were getting out of hand. There was wild talk of changing society – a revolution.

An ungrateful parliament ordered the army to disband and go home, without pay. In disgust, Cromwell decided to act. He rode away from London and on the day he left, a group of soldiers (probably obeying his orders) seized the king.

■ KILLING THE KING ■

THE SOLDIERS KEPT the king prisoner at Hampton Court Palace. In June 1647, Cromwell rode there to talk to the king. Meeting Charles for the first time, he decided that the sovereign was foolish rather than wicked. A kind father himself, Cromwell was touched to see how much Charles missed his children.

PARLIAMENT AND ARMY

Parliament and the army were now in open disagreement. At one point, Fairfax was ready to lead the army to Westminster and close down parliament. But Cromwell insisted that parliament must stay. He still hoped for a peaceful settlement.

Then came news that the king had escaped and fled to the Isle of Wight. Cromwell was angry, and doubly so when he learned that Charles was now asking for help from the Scots.

Cromwell's son-in-law, Henry Ireton, spoke out. Charles must go. Cromwell too decided that the country would be better off without the king.

A SECOND WAR

The second Civil War which began in 1648 was short, consisting mainly of a series of Royalist uprisings. The Scots raised an army to fight for Charles, but on 17 August, Cromwell defeated the Scottish army at Preston. Parliament was triumphant.

EVENTS

1647 The parliamentary army is all but disbanded. The king escapes but is recaptured.
1648 Thirty Years' War ends with the Treaty of Westphalia. Half the people of Germany have died in the war. The Scots begin Second Civil War. The Dutch Republic becomes independent from Spanish rule. An uprising in France, known as the Fronde, takes place. In England, a preacher named George Fox founds the Society of Friends (Quakers).
1649 Charles I is executed. England becomes a Commonwealth.

VOTES FOR ALL

THE LEVELLERS were a group of people who looked for drastic changes in England. They wanted to 'level men's estates' – to make all men equal. Another group, known as the Diggers, began digging up waste ground and planting vegetables, saying that poor people had the right to land stolen from them by the rich. Such ideas were attacked in print (right) but alarmed landowners like Cromwell. The Leveller leader John Lilburne was arrested and kept in prison until 1655.

▼ King Charles was tried for treason in Westminster Hall, London. He was not allowed to answer the charges against him.

▶ On 30 January 1649, Charles I was beheaded on a block set up outside the Banqueting House in Whitehall. He met his death bravely in front of the watching crowds.

◀ The warrant (order) for Charles I's execution. Among those who signed it were Cromwell and his son-in-law Henry Ireton.

Warrant to Execute King Charles the First. A.D. 1648.

THE KING'S TRIAL

In January 1649, the army forced parliament to set up a court to try the king. Charles retorted that no court had the power to bring him to trial. Nevertheless, the trial went ahead, in Westminster Hall in London.

The king was found guilty of treason. Cromwell was one of the parliamentary leaders who signed the order for the king's death. On 30 January 1649, Charles I was executed. His head was cut off with an axe in front of a crowd outside the Palace of Whitehall in London.

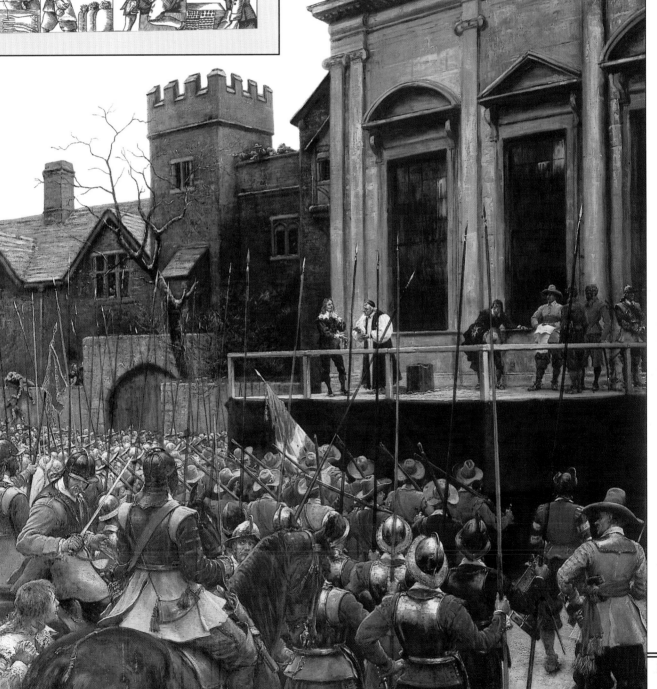

■ CROMWELL IN IRELAND ■

IN 1649 CROMWELL led an army to Ireland. The English had been fighting in Ireland on and off for 500 years in an effort to conquer it but had always met with fierce opposition. Most Irish people were Roman Catholics. During Elizabeth I's reign, England had tried to make Ireland a Protestant country. The English took land from the Irish and gave it to Protestant settlers (known as 'planters') from England and Scotland. The Irish resented the settlers and often attacked them. A major rebellion began in 1641, with the Catholics claiming the support of Charles I.

ENGLISH REVENGE

Cromwell was determined to put an end to the Irish rebellion. Parliament feared that Ireland might be used as a

EVENTS

1607 After the flight of the earls of Tyrone and Tyrconnell from Ireland, the English government seizes their lands and gives them to 'planters' from England and Scotland.
1641 Catholics in Ireland revolt and kill thousands of Protestants. The fighting continues for the next ten years.
1646 Owen Roe O'Neill wins a battle at Benburb.
1649 Cromwell's army massacres people in Drogheda and Wexford.
1650 Cromwell returns to Ireland.

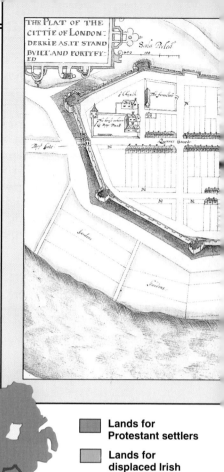

▶ Cromwell's policy in Ireland was 'thorough'. In several towns his troops slaughtered soldiers and townspeople alike, as well as any Catholic priests found. Irish landowners were banished to Connaught and their estates divided among Cromwell's soldiers. Catholic worship was banned and priests went into hiding.

Lands for Protestant settlers

Lands for displaced Irish

✕ Towns stormed by Cromwell

Londonderry
ULSTER
Sligo
Castlebar
CONNAUGHT
Drogheda ✕
Dublin
LEINSTER
Carlow ✕
Limerick
Kilkenny ✕
Carrick ✕
Ross ✕
Clonmel ✕
MUNSTER
Wexford ✕
Cork

◀▲ The siege of Drogheda. This unfinished sketch shows women and children on the barricades, while (above) Cromwell and his officers watch the bombardment. Because the citizens would not surrender, Cromwell's army stormed the town and killed large numbers of ordinary people.

LIFE IN IRELAND

THE PEOPLE IN Ireland were very poor. They often went hungry because much of the land was too boggy to grow good crops. They were also attacked by local leaders, or chieftains, fighting among themselves. The best land was taken by English and Scottish settlers. The Irish were Catholics, but the settlers were Protestants. After Cromwell's campaign of 1649, the Catholics lost even more rights. The English government divided up the provinces of Ulster, Leinster and Munster among Cromwell's soldiers, reducing the amount of land owned by Catholics from 60 per cent to about 20 per cent.

◀ In an area of Ireland still troubled today, the City of London took land for settlers and renamed the city of Derry, Londonderry.

▲ Henry Ireton fought in Ireland with Cromwell, his father-in-law. In 1650, he captured Carlow and Waterford, but died of the plague the following year during the siege of Limerick.

base for an invasion of England by Royalists or foreign enemies such as Spain or France.

At the town of Drogheda, Cromwell called on the Royalist commander to surrender, but he refused. Angry Roundhead soldiers broke through the walls and Cromwell did nothing to stop their savagery. Townspeople, including Catholic priests, were mercilessly slaughtered. A few weeks later the citizens of Wexford were also put to the sword. By the end of 1649, Cromwell had left Ireland, but the massacres left a legacy of anger and hatred. Cromwell returned in 1650, but the Irish went on fighting for two more years. The country was now even more wretched and many Irish soldiers left to fight in the armies of France or Spain. Catholic Ireland was crushed.

◀ James Butler, Duke of Ormonde, commanded the Protestant Royalist army in Ireland. During the Civil War he surrendered Dublin to parliament and fled to join Royalist exiles in France. At the Restoration (1660), he was made Lord Lieutenant of Ireland by Charles II.

■ THE COMMONWEALTH ■

$\mathbf{A}$FTER THE EXECUTION of Charles I, England was a republic for the first and only time in its history. It was named the Commonwealth. The House of Lords was abolished. In the Rump Parliament (all that was left of the Long Parliament), Cromwell was chairman of the Council of State, a new ruling body.

CROMWELL'S CAMPAIGNS

Cromwell had crushed rebellion in Ireland. Next he defeated the Scots at Dunbar in 1650. In 1651 at Worcester, he defeated the army of Charles II, the son of the dead king. For the time being, the Royalists gave up hope of putting the young king on his father's throne.

Cromwell also dealt firmly with people like the Levellers, who wanted general revolution, and a breakdown of the old rules. He wanted peace and gradual reform, but thought parliament was corrupt and slow to act. In 1653, he did what Charles I had done before him – he dismissed parliament.

EVENTS

1650 *Charles I's son lands in Scotland where he has been hailed as King Charles II. Cromwell defeats the Scots at Dunbar.*
1651 *Cromwell defeats Charles II's army at Worcester. Charles flees to France. Navigation Act introduced to protect English trade.*
1652 *English at war with the Dutch. First coffee house opens in London.*
1653 *Cromwell becomes lord protector.*

▲ Cromwell's disciplined army defeated the Scots force that fought at Dunbar in 1650 in support of Charles II, their newly declared king.

1651

■ Parliament
■ Royalists

◀ The young Charles II was badly beaten in battle at Worcester in 1651. Afterwards he fled to France, dressed as a servant. At one point, so the story goes, he hid in an oak tree while Cromwell's soldiers searched the house in which he had been hiding.

CROMWELL'S ENGLAND

$\mathbf{S}$UCCESSIVE monarchs had feared attack from Ireland, Scotland and elsewhere in Europe. Cromwell's military and naval strength allowed England a period of peace and prosperity. Between 1649 and 1651 Cromwell re-equipped the navy with 40 great warships carrying heavy guns. Under their protection, English merchants sailed the seas unhindered and England's enemies were cautious. At home taxes were high but Cromwell appointed good judges and saw to it that schools and colleges flourished. Ordinary people now had the chance to become generals, admirals, civil servants, scientists and diplomats.

▶ The picture shows a naval architect displaying a model of a new warship.

GOD'S CHOSEN

Cromwell had decided, reluctantly, that God had chosen him to lead the country. He marched into the House of Commons with 30 soldiers, and hustled out the members. Cromwell pointed to the mace, the Speaker's symbol of authority, and asked, 'What shall we do with this bauble? Here, take it away'. So ended the rule of parliament, for which the war had been fought and for which the king had lost his life.

In 1653 Cromwell was made lord protector of England, Scotland and Ireland. He was now king in all but name.

▶ Cromwell dismisses the Rump Parliament in 1653. This cartoon shows members, led by a wise owl, being chased out by nipping dogs, and the Speaker by armed men. Written on the wall is 'This House is to Let'. Cromwell replaced this parliament with the short-lived Barebones Parliament, made up of non-elected 'godly' Puritans.

■ LORD PROTECTOR ■

A S LORD PROTECTOR, Cromwell was more tolerant than many of his Puritan followers. He thought people should be free to practise their own religion in private. He allowed Jews to return to England, after a 200-year ban. He wanted fairer judges, for he did not think it right that a man should be hanged for stealing a purse.

In private, Cromwell was less stern than he seemed in public. He enjoyed music and watching young people dancing at weddings, and was fond of a pipe of tobacco and a glass of beer. He was happiest with his family, laughing at their practical jokes.

UNRULY PARLIAMENTS

Parliament gave him little time for family life. Cromwell called two parliaments to help govern the country, but could not control them. Some MPs wanted to do away with the Church of England altogether. They passed laws banning

EVENTS

1654 *Russia at war with Poland. Otto von Guericke, a German scientist, makes the first air pump.*
1655 *Cromwell dismisses his first parliament. England is split into 11 military districts. England captures Jamaica from Spain. Sweden and Poland go to war.*
1656 *England and Spain fight a war (until 1659). Charles X of Sweden wins the battle of Warsaw against the Poles.*
1657 *The first pendulum clock is made by Christiaan Huygens of Holland.*
1658 *Cromwell dismisses his second parliament, and governs England without it.*

GOING TO SCHOOL

C ROMWELL believed in better education and set new standards for teachers. He was chancellor of Oxford University and founded a college at Durham. Students at

◀ Cromwell, the lord protector – king in all but name.

▼ Mrs Cromwell lived quietly and, as she assured Charles II after his Restoration, took little part in her husband's political or military affairs. She knew nothing about His Majesty's missing jewels!

▲ Puritanism flourished in the New World. Jamestown, Virginia, the first permanent English settlement in America, was Puritan but became a royal colony in 1624. Here, the colonists join forces with ministers of the Commonwealth.

university (above) and boys at grammar schools learnt Latin and Greek, history, some mathematics, a little science, and divinity. Poor children were lucky to go to school at all. Girls were taught at home, learning to read, draw, sew, cook and run a household.

Christmas celebrations, plays and public dancing. New laws made swearing and drunkenness punishable by death.

Cromwell tried splitting the country into districts governed by army generals, but that was unpopular. In 1657, parliament offered him the chance to be king, but he refused.

FOREIGN POLICY

Cromwell tried to make England the leader of the Protestant nations of Europe. He built up a strong navy, and after beating the Dutch at sea, made peace with them. He also made friendly alliances with Sweden and Denmark.

Jamaica, in the West Indies, was won as a colony from Spain in 1655. With the help of France, a Catholic country, Cromwell's forces also defeated the Spanish at Dunkirk in 1658. For a time, Dunkirk became an English possession.

▲ Once poachers in England risked hanging. Cromwell was against harsh punishments for such petty crimes. Only murder, treason and rebellion deserved death.

▼ Parliament tried to make everyone live by Puritan standards. No cock-fighting, horse-racing or Sunday sports were allowed. Drinking and gambling in taverns were no pastimes for godly citizens.

■ THE DEATH OF CROMWELL ■

CROMWELL WAS a fond father. When his favourite daughter Betty died in July 1658, he was heartbroken. He had been in poor health since returning from Ireland and was now suffering from malaria. He was taken to London, where he died on 3 September 1658.

A STRANGE FUNERAL

Cromwell's death came as a shock to his friends and supporters. They arranged a grand state funeral. The procession took seven hours to reach Westminster Abbey. A wax figure of the lord protector was on show. But Cromwell's body had been buried in secret 10 days earlier.

AFTER CROMWELL

Cromwell's son, Richard, became the new lord protector, but he was not up to such high office and resigned. In 1660

RESTORATION DIARY

SAMUEL Pepys (1633-1703) was educated at the same school as Cromwell and admired his school's most famous old boy. Pepys studied at Cambridge University and went on to hold an important position in the navy board and to become a member of parliament. But he is most famous for the Diary he wrote. In this he describes his colourful daily life alongside important events, including the Restoration. He tells about the theatre and musical performances, the latest advances in science, the gossip at court and the comings and goings of all kinds of people.

◀ **Richard Cromwell, the new lord protector, did not want to rule England. The army did not want him either.**

▲ The execution of the regicides (those who had signed Charles I's death warrant). Ten of the 28 accused were hanged, drawn and quartered. The rest were jailed for life.

General Monck, commander of the army, allowed elections. The new parliament sent a message to France. It invited Charles II, living in exile there, to return as king. In the spring of 1660, crowds cheered the new king as he travelled from Dover to London. The Commonwealth was over.

Cromwell was dishonoured as a traitor. His body, which had been embalmed, was taken from its tomb and hung up at Tyburn, London's place of execution for criminals. His head was stuck on a pole above Westminster Hall, where it remained for years.

▼ Charles II's coronation procession. The king wanted to bring his people together again after the divisions of the Civil War and Commonwealth.

■ CROMWELL'S LEGACY ■

UNDER CROMWELL, Puritan beliefs took hold in England. Bishops were no longer allowed in the Church of England and people chose their own church ministers. Because Puritans disliked 'frivolities', the theatres were closed – but not for long. After the Restoration of Charles II, bishops and theatres returned.

For ordinary people, life under Cromwell – and after him – went on much as before. Most were glad to have peace again after the Civil War. Cromwell had few firm ideas about how his country should be governed. He had fought the king because he believed the king had taken too much power into his own hands. By a twist of fate, the death of the king left Cromwell with even greater powers of his own.

Cromwell ruled because he believed God told him to. He was most at ease with his soldiers, and he helped to create a strong and well-organized army, a model for future armies. He also improved the navy. This was important for the future of Britain as a trading nation with overseas colonies.

After years of upheaval and war, Oliver Cromwell made England strong and respected. His statue stands outside the Houses of Parliament in London. For, after Cromwell, no king ever tried to challenge the rule of parliament as Charles I had done.

HARD TIMES FOR PURITANS

CHARLES II was a Protestant, but he disliked the Puritanism of Cromwell's time. During his reign, Puritan religious services were forbidden and Puritans banned from government jobs. Puritan preachers were locked up. A Puritan pot-mender named

A MOVING LETTER

CROMWELL (right) is seen by some as an inhuman figure, but his humanity is apparent in this letter of sympathy to his brother-in-law Valentine Walton, after the death of Walton's son at Marston Moor. In it, Cromwell refers to his own eldest son's death.

'Sir, God hath taken away your eldest son by a cannon shot. It brake his leg. We were necessitated to have it cut off, wherof he died . . . Sir, you know my trials this way; but the Lord supported me with this, that the Lord took him into the happiness we all pant after and live for.'

▼ Along with many other places of entertainment, London's Globe theatre was closed by the Puritans.

Theatrical performances were allowed after 1660, but fewer ordinary people went to them.

John Bunyan (below) was sent to prison for preaching without a licence and there wrote his famous book, *The Pilgrim's Progress*. The poet John Milton (left) had been editor of the Commonwealth's chief newspaper and, in fiercely argued pamphlets, had defended 'the good old cause'. Now blind, the poet wrote in despair that Charles II's return marked the end of freedom and the return of slavery.

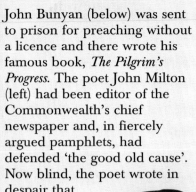

▶ Cromwell's statue outside the Houses of Parliament, London. After Cromwell no king dared to challenge the rule of parliament as Charles I had done.

▶ How many more? In Ireland, where Cromwell's brutality still causes bitterness, a minority of Catholic nationalists and Protestant loyalists are still prepared to fight.

◀ The official messenger Black Rod knocks three times on the door of the House of Commons to summon MPs to attend the monarch in the House of Lords for the opening of parliament. The door is slammed in his face in a ritual that reasserts the supremacy of the House of Commons.

■ GLOSSARY ■

APPRENTICE Young man learning a trade or craft by working for an experienced tradesman.

ARMADA Invasion fleet sent by Spain against England in 1588.

CATHOLIC A follower of the Christian faith who obeys the teachings of the Roman Catholic Church and its head, the pope.

CAVALIER A supporter of the Royalists.

CAVALRY Soldiers mounted on horses.

CIVIL WAR War between different groups within a country.

COLONY Settlement founded overseas.

COMMONWEALTH Name chosen by parliament to describe England under Cromwell.

CUDGEL Heavy stick used for fighting or mock-fights.

DISSOLVE (of parliament) To break up; send the members of parliament home.

DIVINE RIGHT Belief that a ruler has a God-given right to rule that cannot be challenged.

EMBALM To preserve a dead body so that it keeps a life-like appearance.

GRAMMAR SCHOOL A town school, not run by the church.

HAWKING Using trained hawks to hunt for game as a sport (or for food).

HUNTING Chasing and killing animals for sport (or for food).

INFANTRY Foot soldiers.

LAWYER Person trained in law.

LEVELLER Person who wanted extreme changes in society, including free land.

LORD PROTECTOR Title given to Cromwell as sole ruler of England.

MEMBER OF PARLIAMENT Someone who is elected to serve in the House of Commons.

MERCHANT Person who buys and sells goods.

MONARCHY System of government in which the head of state is a king or queen.

MUSKET Hand gun with a long barrel, often rested on a stand when it was fired.

PAMPHLET Booklet printed and distributed to put forward an argument or point of view.

PARLIAMENT Elected assembly of people. In Cromwell's time, only a few men could vote to elect members of parliament.

PERSECUTION Unfair or cruel treatment of people.

PIKE Weapon with a very long handle and spear-like pointed tip.

POLITICS The business of power and government.

PROTESTANTS Christians who broke away from the Catholic Church during the Reformation to set up their own churches.

PURITANS People who practised a simple form of Christian worship, without ornaments or ceremony in churches, and also lived simply.

RADICAL Person who seeks extreme or dramatic changes in society.

REBELLION Uprising against the government or those in power.

REVOLUTION Violent upheaval to overthrow old ways and rules.

REPUBLIC System of government in which the head of state is elected, and not a monarch.

ROUNDHEAD Supporter of parliament during the Civil War, so named because many (such as boy apprentices) had short hair.

ROYALIST Supporter of King Charles I and his son, later Charles II.

SIEGE Attack on a castle or walled town by an army which surrounds it to stop help getting in or the defenders getting out.

SPEAKER Impartial spokesperson, chosen by the House of Commons, whose duties include making sure that members act properly.

TAVERN Inn or public house.

TOLERANCE Believing that people of all religious faiths or none should be treated fairly.

TREASON Crime of plotting against the good of the state, the government or a ruler.

VOLUNTEERS People who willingly join an activity or organization.

BATTLES AND BATTLEFIELDS

First Civil War
Edgehill 1642

Lansdown 1643

Roundway Down 1643

Calgrove Field 1643

Newbury (first battle) 1643

Cheriton 1644

Nantwich 1644

Marston Moor 1644

Newbury (Second battle) 1644

Naseby 1645

Second Civil War
Preston 1648

Dunbar 1650

Worcester 1651

Ireland
Drogheda 1649

Wexford 1649

PLACES TO VISIT

The Banqueting House, Whitehall, London.

Caernarfon Castle, Gwynedd.

Chepstow Castle, Monmouthshire.

Claydon House, Buckinghamshire.

The Commandery Civil War Centre, Sidbury, Worcestershire.

Conwy Castle, Conwy.

Corfe Castle, Dorset.

Cromwell Museum, Huntingdon.

Denbigh Castle, Denbighshire.

Donnington Castle, Berkshire.

Edgehill Battle Museum, Warwickshire.

Harlech Castle, Gwynedd.

King Charles Tower, Chester.

Marston Moor Battlefield, Yorkshire.

Naseby Battlefield, Leicestershire.

Newbury Museum, Berkshire.

Oxford Museum.

Scone Palace, Perth.

Tower of London.

Wardour Old Castle, Wiltshire.

Warwick Castle.

York Castle Museum.

Information of interest may also be obtained from these organizations:

The Cromwell Association, Croswell Cottage, Northedge, Tupton, Chesterfield S42 6AY.

The English Civil War Society, 70 Hallgate, Howden DN14 7ST.

The Sealed Knot, 58 Hearthway, Banbury OX16 7QP.
This society re-creates bygone battles with its members wearing uniforms and carrying weapons modelled on those originally used.

■ INDEX ■